SOMEBODY PLEASE

POEMS

DAVE BARRETT

Blue Arrangements
Salem, MA, USA
1st Edition, 2026
Cover design by Susan Carroll
Typeset by Calvin Cummings

Typset in Chakra Petch and Legitima.

"A book of aphoristic wit meant to be read in bouts of coughing laughter or sung to the cold night skies."

— Graham Irvin, author of *I Have a Gun*

"Here is a poet. To think we're all working with the same tools..."

— Lamb

SOMEBODY PLEASE

POEMS

DAVE BARRETT

SOMEBODY PLEASE

Somebody please squeeze eden from a mighty tree

AUTHORITY

he asked me like a butterfly
and I answered him like a felon
stealing from the air
ultimate power

his authority
had a trace of desperation
for my preview
he cradled each question

he asked me like a mother
he asked me nicely
and patiently like a motherfucker

EVERYTHING

I tried to pretend
I heard everything
and nodded my head
repeatedly
obsequiously
and like a chameleon
my color changed back
to its original
vantage point green

DO I NEED ANOTHER ONE

I love the idea of making mistakes in heaven

I AM SO HEARTBROKEN

I can shape phantasm into bombast
and find places fleshy and bulbous with words
in the brain where metal misbehaves

I am so heartbroken
I want to arrest you with my disappointment

I want you to get why
a poem doesn't need to be perfect
to shatter your skull

A GRIP SO SMALL

sometimes when I'm stuck
I take any random old book
and open to any random old page

and find

his fingers burned
or
the firmest proof

see how it fits
into
a grip so small

I moused at asking the hard questions and really didn't want to sneak around as a fluke of nature wailing away with a chance

MELANCHOLY OAK

something naughtycal
about the wood from my bed

like an old slaver

it's not the sinking torment
responsibility for them
to treat the timber
but for you to smoothen the grooves
and make something musical
from the melancholy

INSTEAD OF DOUBT

if I only knew then
how to unclamp my fingers
from prying into her soil

watch the intrigue hatch
from the pendulous silence
of her own way

faith knows
how to make the answers grow right
from the garden of our hands

RODE STIFF

I scribbled rod and staff

one night

the next day

rode stiff
instead

god
get laid

SICKER

finally

I couldn't tell
the difference

between all that
and all that
blue

WITH THE LYRICS SHE SPOKE

with the lyrics
she spoke

and with that first meow
owned everything I would ever earn
in my entire life

she was like a character in a movie
I paid many times to see
but my dad was a dog guy
so I got half price
and in the spring summer and fall
she would have to sometimes fend for herself
but he figured in the cold cage of winter
even the most thoreau of animals
need a key

like a lot of people who are saved

AFTER I WAS ON THE VERGE

only after I was on the verge
of irreversible decay
did we find a way to bleed out
the trauma from the gums
and follow enough thin instruction
from the winnowing roots
to help me stop grinding
on the bones of a false story
years of wearing
the crowns of adulthood

BID LITTLE JABBER

smear the iridescent venom
the coral flexes for a rounder truth
hoist your unlikely bid little jabber
there's nobody teaching the tiny

the grass warps away with edges free
hook bent trains whine into the corn
a tired queen of dairy longs for a cooler sleep
this stiffened sky is an old and tempered meat

NOW

like first flesh before the bell bird shy

NOW SUMMER GROWS

walking to school as a boy
birds would shit cold down on my head
slowing me like security at the airport
during puberty I wiped the icy looking jizz
off the country of my stomach with white socks
as an adult for laughs I pissed on an archbishop's grave
during Halloween night to impress some friends
and soon after was placed in an institution

now summer grows older sooner

and now at 50
I've trapped
the dream of delivering
seed

or the next or the next or the next
every move
and into that
there is no privacy

GOD TO THE ODD

I imagine him
having a taste for me

from appetizer embryo
to a slime of whey
I imagine him
throughout the courses of my life

friends and family next
sloshing the hard bone
in his open mouth
wet chunks
on his chin

but until that day

I AM YOURS

with all the patience
of a summer vine
lift me up
in blossoms
bandaged

ONE SCRUPULOUS FORK

one scrupulous fork is all it takes
to break the hubris of your airplane apart
like pot roast and dip the juicy helpings
into the neutral history of the sea

and if you've been spared or not
death as much as a brain
makes the spirit shake
the balance of salt out
from the dispersing mist
and seasons the harvest
of meaty waves
with taste

WHAT A GREAT HOME CAN TEACH

that was her speaking up when she absolutely had to
teaching me about the kitchens of winter
the dry furry holes
the greatest need to defend them
the bossy rabbits and their perfect white coats
the ordering of new tests you don't need
the biological prerogative of what makes an icebox hum

and it shouldn't be any fancier than that
if the moisture of love is lacking
if the kisses aren't kicking
if an unchained melody can't shed the tension away
if for any other reason or no reason
she simply says no

IT HELPS ME

it helps me to think of god as a clown

SOLACE

the soul has forever to explain

SOMETIMES THE NIGHT

sometimes the night
and all that
rich blue diamond light
shrinks
and fits inside
the shell of a seed
tucked away
into a world
most certainly
meant
for me

THANK GOD

thank god

I learned to be
a fish in the flood

the summer I turned 16
watched me
march out of the nerves
of my father's black teeth
and into the awkward smile
of my own manhood

TO CHIMPANZEE

to chimpanzee
these little thoughts
is all it takes
lucky me

THE THREE OF THEM

It felt really good to have another big animal in the room watching over both of them.

THE CURSE

she spoke dirty

dead branches
make good wood

she reckoned me

her dark
crooked place

ruined me

I insisted

THE FREEDOM

miles of loosened tongue with mouths

BLOODY TASTE COMING

nothing will prepare you
for the bloody taste coming
and the raw tang
of knowledge
wrapped tightly
will inevitably leak
and pour out
and you're the strongest
serve yourself first

WHEN EDEN FELL

she tasted each tulip with the tip of her tongue

BLOOM

the flowers joust the night
so that even the most irksome dinner knives
might have a chance with the sharp side down
to unguard her buds with swordplay

THE ORGAN

I never went
to religion classes
or church
but I know
the moxie
of the organ
its shivers
flat and black
cold and white
into the
muscle of me
the keys of its lips
keeps me tasting
the blood
the falling teeth
the scared children
out of the baby
of my mouth

BRIDE

she would just lie there
avoiding me
jigsawed into a thousand
parts
face down
until she made me roll
all of her over
onto her glossy side
and from there I couldn't stop myself
from jamming certain pieces in
as the picture
of what I was putting together
started to appear to me
slowly

THAT ALL DON'T HUNT AFTER

opportunity finds
the wreckage of shame
difficult
but worthy of scavenging
on every ocean and 13th floor
like it was tailored
and plainspoken
with clubbed feet hands
it loves in labor
what it lost

OCCUPIED

she didn't want a treaty
obey the moans of her highway she said
be unsatisfied with the simple candy
she was offering
at the gas station in the town
the father in me wanted to stop at
scream the hostility out of her
despise her beg
undervalue her civility
unsweeten her
with the tools in my kit bag
be her unremarkabler-in-chief
transgress through
the exclusions of her lips
let the black ops of my tongue
drive unmercifully
into the burdens of her mouth
blast and make
every tooth know
the outrage of defeat
and die
already

CHARM

she was the kind who wanted me
and that made me unzip
in the original bouquets
and unneighborly ways
of suspicion
and snake like a lawn
to inveigle her trees

she knew I had something
better than an erection
to reap the soil with
a geyser
to shoot its only hot way
from the smoke of my oneness
into the evolution of her voice

though everything is dry now
like a dust that must settle
into the morgue of its last vacant shape
though even the moon has ancillary plans
I can still float on a wavy day
and soak like salt to skin

PRAYER

to guide
the prominence
of words
into the forest
of the ear
each dropping vowel
each disappearing syllable
reasonable

THE FIDDLE WAS IN THE FUN

as a child
I knew the fiddle was in the fun
and though I fooled
in the stutter of my steps
like a sultan of swing
I saw behind the rules
and stood waiting
for the turns of the wind
to suggest

CALL

we can groan
privately on islands
and lay in the odors of our sand
until the pacified nobody
of waves and winds
helps us climb out of our minds
and carries us back
to that most returned to place

CRETINOUS MISTAKE

a lip is a lip
a hand is a hand
and in the dark morning
prophecy is a breakfast
of winter oats
that clenches the jaw
so no amount of bite can chew
its hard words into a bolus
so unable
to mush and mill
these grains of fate
no right amount of milk
softens the shame
of their cretinous mistake
into a rich bowl of protein

DESCENT

I didn't see
how a bull's grunt
could inhabit my face
with such authority

and so I never hindered
my terrible lows
against
the ceaseless dolor
of the herd

HE SAID I WAS UNABLE

he said I was unable
to tell a good story of my past
that the memories were
stuck in the cold and old
regions of the brain
and that was how it went
until we opened a place

OLD KING AND DOG

I was never so afraid
as when I saw foamy phrases
frothed like a nation seceding
from old king and dog

ONE FLIGHT UP

even the most
lordly of roots
that prosper
into the wealth of trees
need no witness
like their human cousins
to shew the shine
of their feat

PRAISE TO THE ODD

dormant
buds

in trunks
of kings

tease the burl
out

from crowded
wood

SKINNYABLE

an older attractive skinnyable woman
was deftly bagging and paying
for a season's amount of groceries

the he man bagger who was helping her
and the clerk who was checking her out
asked if she needed help
putting them in her car
and she said no to their offer

and after purchasing my one item
milk of course
I saw her again
when she asked
if I needed help

SURE

we dry humped
in desperate
and cemented themes
with cheeky tongues
we poked like pigs

THE WEDDING BREAKFAST

her unambiguous aromas
gave him enough may to unstick
from the gravy of bad ideas
high into the salvage and marvel
of her eggs and biscuits

ELEMENTARY

there are days
when even the ants
seem murderous
running backwards
like time
away from maturity
effective
in their own
ruthless nest
drunk
like flies
on their own sense
of lord
biting everything
that doesn't belong
in their 8th grader world
they wrest the weak
from the dead
with no clue
of the ghosts
that might follow
with their own
insulting
report card

FAMOUS RECIPE

she called him her gassy giant
the calibrations of sperm she teased like an astronaut
rocketing was an unrecoverable equation
how many backpacks of puss
to make that slug of white gravy

FROM MOONY STONES

from moony stones and glassy wishes
the hands and feet of my dreams
are evolving

the old humps sitting crooked
on the sand bar of my throat like relics
have been freed with dumb hiccups

everything that was funny
now reminds me I'm ready to leave
for the heave and buck of the deep

I've been child to this master long enough
in the easy bay of fusty words suburban leisures
instruct the mad ladies of right now

to leverage this nubbly little boat of grunts and sighs
against the clean sheets of white sense
and face the dogsleeped wind and slaughtered stock
of tomorrow's waves

GENIUS

the genius of children turns fact into riddle

WHICH PARENT

with a framed look that was meant to hang there above
mother don't be a cunt

SWITCH

calmly
behind the potential
of each generation
is a switch
that turns
my
family portrait
of unsmiling faces
me

MY LITTLE HANDS

my little hands
fussed over what looked like a giant pot of chili
as she groaned back into her towel
she cooked from under me and I cooked from above
me dripping sweat into the oil only made it hotter
and because she wasn't angry she pulled me in deeper
like a little shaver into the colder and older and less unsubtle parts
and baited me almost like a patient to proceed
the mouth of her ass so massively shut
it seemed to be responsible for everything
and hidden from my view at the same time
with my little eyes and thighs
wrapped around her calf
all of what was illegal I dared not touch
but grabbed for anyway instead
and all she did was let out a little yelping sound
that was not part of the body I knew
and then she said no
not there

GOODY

as a boy I got my first erections
at sea
when girl babysitters
kissed me on the cheeks
and let me crash into their reefs

I also sailed proud
when I saw
pictures of giants
eating things
smaller

HIM TOO

I know it's not the same
but I too know what it's like
to misremember a memory
claw without a clue
hide in the hungry
muff in the mouth

no period
no pressure
no poem
no poise

not even
like a hero pretending

IF YOU'VE EVER DARED TO LOVE

knowing I might hump your skull
nothing lets me in like an open mind
every piece of gossip is worth listening to

IN ITS SLOW

chin melting music and easy bruise of truth
pulled the sagging skin off his face

IN THE PRESENCE OF MOTHER

pages of snow are
suckled to the wet trees
okay a lot is allowed to die

LIKE THEIR BUTTS WEREN'T IN IT

at the graveyard where the ground was sweating
the birds came in to splash
memories crawled into the immersed sigh of our adieu
she looked worm and waterproof peaceful
kissing the wood
she'd kiss the bugs too if she could
I wanted the coffin to slide
plunge and swagger like a ship
but the land was sober and nobody screamed
everyone spoke prayers like their butts weren't in it
I had the words there
it seemed exactly like I should
could
and then when I finally did I didn't and then I did again
and it was like in second grade
I felt that large breasted imposed upon feeling
closing in on my breath
the sky mothered its woodpecker chance
and the drilling began

LOSE NOT THY NATURE

not everything great
has a place in line to wait
for the last culled slabs of tougher meat
to cook in the impartial ovens of time
until huge tender chunks finally pull away
from those silky glaciers of fat

MUSKY

I felt her cardinal thrust of roots
her thin smell stayed
in the breath of short weeds

MY PILL

I translate old pain written on rock

WHAT A BREEZE

I would chase her
if I could catch her
that would be a sign
it's easy to see now
if she got away

PRAYER

a voice
hits the licorice nail
in your mind
he needs you
sweetened

REBEL

in the videos I saw in mid tear
the rock of his shoulders
being robbed from his face

the smile
slowly
dislocating

into a pain somewhere
so impossible

a father
could never see

but a generation could

THE YOUNG

that's the young
masculine
face of morning
jittery and speculating
in the crowded stadiums
of risk
where he was first placed
under the strict tutelage of context
and later became as eager
as other dawns before him

THE BLUE HERON

she was staring into the water like a monk
who's watching me?

THE WHISPERING

the whispering
at some basic level
maybe its just a hunch
helps another
helps another
helps another
helps another
helps another
helps another
helps another
helps another
adds up

THESE THINGS FORBIDDEN

even on pluto I can still access the internet
some signal from some carrier's high heaven
bring me scraps of porn I use to gobble away at

unwilling to concede
and vagabond the drugs I will always have to take
because god

sealed in the inches of his philanthropy
lets the right medicine unscrew from his own twisted capsules
for even the most leastful creatures

so that I too may be allowed to imagine these things forbidden
in the honey rich moon forgotten waters
of my isolation

UNTREASURED

before the meds
came like a porn star
all over the humanity
of my face
I would hit
the ceiling with tears
something like
the opposite
of orgasm
would ejaculate
slow like a century
out of the history of me
and leave me
so untreasured
with no option
but to gulp limply
at the bushels of air
like a dirty puppy
not even somebody else's
olympus mother and father
could take me
into the mercy of their chest
and tug away the pain
from the bruised nipples
of my little world

VIRGIN

I used to blush
when someone
used the word white
like they were stealing
my history away from me
like somehow they
were going to find out
my embarrassing secrets
and break all the bulbs
in my closet

ACKNOWLEDGEMENTS

The following poems first appeared in NOON

SOMEBODY PLEASE (2020)

WHAT I DID (2020)

THE THREE OF THEM (2021)

I'd like to thank Diane Williams for her encouragement

ALSO FROM *BLUE ARRANGEMENTS*

Cheap Seats by Kayla Jean

Everything Happens Next by Will Stanier

Boys Nite by Ty Healey

To purchase, visit **bluearrangements.com**
or email **lazysusan.blue@gmail.com**

www.ingramcontent.com/pod-product-compliance
Lightning Source LLC
Chambersburg PA
CBHW031757150726
47989CB00006B/2756